CELTIC CROSSES
COLORING BOOK

CARI BUZIAK

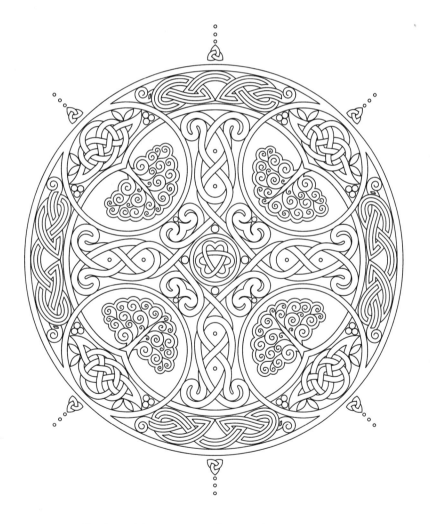

DOVER PUBLICATIONS, INC.
MINEOLA, NEW YORK

Revered for its Christian and Irish symbolism, the Celtic cross is a common motif in jewelry, art, and beyond. This beautiful gallery of intricately drawn Celtic crosses features Irish symbols like harps and shamrocks, as well as objects found in nature, including trees, leaves, flowers, and birds. The interweaving patterns are set against a variety of circular and rectangular backgrounds. Just select your media and experiment with the colors of your choice as you enjoy the artistic possibilities of this unique collection—plus, the perforated, unbacked pages make displaying your work easy!

Bibliographical Note

Celtic Crosses Coloring Book is a new work, first published by Dover Publications, Inc., in 2018.

International Standard Book Number

ISBN-13: 978-0-486-82668-4
ISBN-10: 0-486-82668-6

Manufactured in the United States by LSC Communications
82668601   2018
www.doverpublications.com